C000108853

EXPLORING THE
SECRET WORLD
OF WILDLIFE RESCUE

EXPLORING THE
SECRET WORLD
OF WILDLIFE RESCUE

HELPING HANDS FOR WILDLIFE

Compiled and edited by Pauline Kidner

Best Wishes
from
Pauline K
2012

SWWR
SECRET WORLD
wildlife rescue

HALSGROVE

First published in Great Britain in 2003
Reprinted 2004

Opening title page: *Nothing too small – baby weasel* Photograph: Colin Seddon

Copyright© 2003 Pauline Kidner

*All rights reserved. No part of this publication may be reproduced,
stored in a retrieval system, or transmitted in any form or by any means
without the prior permission of the copyright holder.*

British Library Cataloguing-in-Publication Data
A CIP record for this title is available from the British Library

ISBN: 1 84114 316 2

HALSGROVE

Halsgrove House
Lower Moor Way
Tiverton, Devon EX16 6SS
Tel: 01884 243242
Fax:01884 243325
email: sales@halsgrove.com
website: www.halsgrove.com

Printed by D'Auria Industrie Grafiche Spa, Italy

Foreword

Increasingly, wildlife relies on gardens as habitats and it is great that so many people are prepared to have that secluded area to attract a variety of mammals and birds. However, such close proximity means that, all too often, the realisation that a creature is in need of care can cause a problem.

Thank heavens that people like the staff and volunteers at Secret World are prepared to help at any time and go to extraordinary lengths, with the aim of returning each casualty back to the wild. This book catalogues the creation of a wildlife rescue centre that is nationally acclaimed for its work.

Founder Pauline Kidner has been seen many times on television, walking badger cubs, feeding roe kids in the kitchen or nursing tiny baby bats as small as your thumbnail. You will be amazed at the beautiful photographs and stories. Sit back and enjoy it in the knowledge that all the royalties from this book will be going to the care work at Secret World Wildlife Rescue.

Alan Titchmarsh
August 2003

Dedication

Nikki Hawkins – fellow kindred spirit – for everything.

© Bernadette McArdle

Acknowledgements

Richard Austin, who over the years has taken the majority of photographs at Secret World, first thought of the idea for this book. As a professional photographer, his patience and flair have resulted in so many pictures that have caught that 'special moment', which has allowed us a great deal of press coverage attracting donations that enable us to carry out our work.

But it would only have been possible with the help and involvement of photographers and celebrities who have donated pictures to document the care of animals at Secret World Wildlife Rescue. I would like to thank each celebrity or photographer who has a section in this book including Alan Titchmarsh who has kindly written the foreword.

Further thanks must go to the following people who have allowed us to use their photographs: Colin Seddon, Colin Fountain, Simon Kidner, David Higgs, Richard Taylor-Jones, Andrew Gel, Peter Coleine, Jeff Searle, Purple Pictures, Dave Newman and Stan Dean.

Contents

David Higgs

An enchanting common dormouse – the only British species of mouse that hibernates. Few people can tell you much about the dormouse, other than it was the one that was always asleep in the teapot in Alice in Wonderland! Also known as the Seven Sleeper as it can sleep for seven months of the year, this small mouse is more likely to be found up in the trees than on the ground.

Pauline and Barney the dog greet Bluebell on her nightly visit.

If you are an animal person, there will always be one animal that will be very special to you in your lifetime – she was mine.

Pauline Kidner

Introduction

Secret World Wildlife Rescue is a special place deep in the heart of Somerset. Originally a small dairy farm, through diversification it became an attraction that was enjoyed by people of all ages. Pauline Kidner's love of animals was to take her on a journey, first as the farmer's wife caring for the calves and lambs that needed that extra bit of attention through to an experienced wildlife rehabilitator.

'It all happened by chance', said Pauline 'once we opened our doors to the public orphaned and injured wildlife seemed to find there way here – a little bit like Noah's Ark!'

Now the charity founder with staff and volunteers aiding this nationally acclaimed rescue centre, Pauline has worked with all different kinds of animals. Through the books that she has written and appearances on television, many people already know about the love and care that is offered to every individual animal that arrives at Secret World.

Celebrities over the years have become involved with this charity and, as is the case for all who have visited, cherish their time spent at Secret World where every casualty is given a second chance. Several sections of this book are dedicated to individual celebrities who share their experiences at this rescue centre and its animals.

This book is a compilation of photographs taken at Secret World, although celebrities have also shared with us some of their favourite pictures that have been taken in other parts of the world. From start to finish, it has an Aaah! factor but more importantly it shows how a team of people can work together for the good of animals, with fantastic results.

Farm Animals

Built in 1675, this farm was originally known as New Road Farm. Who would have imagined at the beginning of the twentieth century, that this was to become a rescue centre for wildlife. Back then, over 30 people worked hard making Cheddar and Caerphilly Cheese and, more importantly… cider!

New Road Farm opened to the public in 1984 and was soon to become Secret World as visitors were to see not only farm animals but also wildlife, enabling them to learn the 'secrets' of the countryside.

Home of Derek and Pauline Kidner with their four children, it is now a special place to the thousands of people who have visited over the years.

Simon Kidner

Photographs: Jason Venus

Above: *Longhorn cow.* *The milking herd of Friesians was sold once the farm diversified and different breeds of cows were kept to show visitors where milk came from.* *So many people did not realise that a cow has to give birth to a calf in order to produce milk.*

Right: *Young Hereford-cross calf, enjoying summer in a butter-cup meadow.*

Simon Kidner

Sausage rolls!

Jason Venus

Matilda and Mildred (daughter), everyone's favourites.

Peter Coleine

The noisy gang – Guinea fowl, and pretty bantam cockerels.

15

Highland cow – Having a bad hair day. You didn't want this cow with her huge horns to swing her head round too quickly to look at what you were doing as you were hand milking!

Jason Venus

Above: *'Don't worry they won't sting you,'* says Mr Sydney Lane, *completely kitted out in a bee-keeper's veil and suit.*

Right: *Proud as a peacock.*

Peter Coleine

Jason Venus

Andy Rouse

Above: *Cuddly Dudley – much loved. The domestic cat kills for fun and is responsible for one-third of our rescue centre's bird casualties and two-thirds of our bat casualties.*

Left: *Wild cat – much maligned but only kills in order to survive.*

Simon Kidner

Barney, the family dog who lived for eighteen years was well known to the visitors – he could recognise a picnic basket from a mile off! Visitors enjoyed meeting the family pets as much as all the others.

Jason Venus

Patron of Secret World
Winner of Wildlife Photographer of the Year 1996

Jason Venus

Secret World: I have known Pauline for many years now, and my first memories are when I met Bluebell and Pauline in the old pig-pens, which later became the observation setts. The work that Pauline and Secret World do is unlike any other I have seen; they go beyond caring for animals, with passion and commitment that always amazes me, even through their toughest of times. I am proud to be part of that commitment and share in the joy that working with animals can bring.

Jason Venus

Doug Woods

Above: *Pauline founded the Bluebell Sett Charity, named after her badger, who, despite having freedom, remained at Secret World throughout her life.*

Left: *Pauline and Bluebell the badger. Bluebell was one of three orphaned badgers that were reared at Secret World in 1989.*

Moroccan Skyline
This was a photograph I took whilst filming with the BBC 'Incredible Journeys' series on TV. We were following the migration path of swallows from England to Africa. The dramatic cloud formation reminds me of the fantastic sights that I saw as I travelled along that journey.

Lizard on the Hill
Whilst working in the Sahara Desert for two weeks, apart from the endless sand dunes there was a surprising amount of lizard activity, this one being almost 3 feet long. I thought a real close wide-angle photograph would give the image scale within its surroundings.

Photographs: Jason Venus

21

Photographs: Jason Venus

Running Badger

Possibly one of my most favourite photographs of all. I have always loved badgers for a long as I can remember. To capture such a stunning image makes all those nights of sitting in the dark and cold worthwhile. The photograph had the added bonus that it won me the title of Wildlife Photographer of the Year in 1996.

Puffin with sand eels
I spent about a week on Skomer island off the Welsh coast. It is not a huge rock, but houses thousands of puffins. Being very brave little birds, they were easy to approach and were very active with young to feed. I was photographing from sun-up to sundown and went through almost 100 rolls of film!

Wildlife

Richard Austin

It has been our privilege over the years to have cared for thousands of animals, always with the aim of returning them to the wild.

Very occasionally we were able to re-home unwanted wild animals that had been kept as pets. In a captive situation wild animals can live very long lives and need lots of care and attention to give them a good quality of life.

Left: *Enjoying his Smarties – Gordon the fox, an unwanted pet was re-homed at Secret World. He was with us for thirteen years.*

Below: *Slowly, because of our obvious love of animals, people began to contact us about orphaned and injured wildlife casualties they had found. Catching them was the first lesson we had to learn. Next was how to care for them. And then, if they recovered, when and how to release them.*

Jason Venus

Jason Venus

Sage the barn owl – a real character, who worked with us for nineteen years promoting the importance of protecting habitats to support these beautiful birds. He attended many shows, schools and book signings and was a firm favourite with all our visitors.

He was to escape whilst in London, staying overnight in a trailer when we went to a show in Hyde Park Corner in 1989. Luckily, he flew onto the shoulder of a policeman during the night, was arrested, spent the night in a prison cell and was returned to us the following day.

Bramble, the first roe-deer kid reared at Secret World by Pauline. After winning the confidence of such a shy and secretive animal, Pauline experienced the joy of sharing early-evening walks with him around the home ground.

It's so hard to when you create a bond with such a lovely creature to eventually give them their freedom. But that's what they want – to be wild and free, and if you love them you'll let them go.

Photographs: Jason Venus

Nutkin the grey squirrel. They may say they're tree rats but they're just adorable and great fun.

Andy Rouse

Grey seal pup – has to be one of the prettiest babies.

Pauline (charity founder), with the family dogs, Sam the Schnauzer, Barney, Heidi the fox, and Sherry the Red Setter. Heidi who lived in the house as a cub, joined the resident foxes in an outside run when she was older. When she was eighteen months old, a wild fox must have taken a fancy to her and chewed the wire from the outside to let her out. We never saw her again – Gordon and Bennet, her fellow inmates decided life was easier on the inside and never took the chance for freedom!

Jason Venus

Simon King

Wildlife film maker and presenter

I first met Pauline Kidner when I wanted to film a young badger searching for grubs. Pauline at that time was rearing her first badger cubs – so it was some time ago! Since then, I have often filmed at Secret World and indeed, a major part of the rearing of barn owl chicks shown in the film 'Tyto the Barn Owl' was taken at their centre.

Their team of staff and volunteers have that enormous stamina, care, commitment, humour and love needed to deal with the many wildlife casualties that are brought in to Secret World Wildlife Rescue. But this charity takes it just that one step further through talks and open days, by educating the public about the need to have things in the right prospective.

For example the lovely barn owls that are everyone's favourite – there are only 9000 in the wild and yet in Britain alone it is estimated that between and 60 and 70,000 pairs are kept in aviaries in captivity. We need people like Pauline and her team to make people aware that the true joy of seeing wildlife is in the countryside, healthy and free.

An exhausting time trying to find enough food for these juvenile barn owl chicks. Each will be eating twice as much as an adult bird.

Jason Venus

Photographs: Jason Venus

Above: *A ball of fluff!*

Right: *Ready to pounce – photographs taken during the production of 'Tyto the Barn Owl' by Simon King. Parts of this wildlife drama were filmed on location at Secret World.*

Photographs: Jason Venus

'Me first mum, me first.' Parent returning to feed the waiting brood.

Beautiful soft feathers that give silent flight.

Garden Birds

Baby birds were the first wildlife orphans to arrive at Secret World and still are a very high proportion of the casualties.

May, June and July are the hectic months at Secret World. The Hospital Room is lined with cage after cage of gaping-mouthed fledglings demanding food every hour from dawn 'til dusk.

We rely very heavily on volunteers to help our experienced staff to cope during this very busy period.

Andy Rouse

Adult male robin.

Photographs: Jason Venus

Above: *Baby robin being hand fed.*

Right: *This is how it should be done – parent bird with ever-demanding family.*

David Higgs

Simon Kidner

Above: *Is it a duckling? Is it a dinosaur? Is it a baby heron? No it's a baby pigeon. This common bird is often not recognised.*

Left: *We always thought we could make a lot of money with this photograph of Nikki and the young thrushes. If we sold it to a pharmaceutical firm – you can just see the billboard poster in the chemist window saying 'problems with thrush? Not if you use …'*

The blue tit – an entertaining visitor to our bird table and not such a popular visitor to our milk bottles!

Desmond Morris

Zoologist, writer and television presenter

Sarah Kennedy and I were not surprised when David Bellamy and Lee Durrell, our judges for the 'Animal Country' award, chose Pauline Kidner as the 1995 winner from a list of excellent finalists.

The clip of a brown hare being released after hours of care during the day and night said it all about the dedication that is required for this kind of work. Having been nurtured from an orphan leveret to finally a strong adult ready to return to the wild meant that Pauline watched it go with mixed emotions. Like a parent watching a child leave home, she was sad for herself but happy for the hare and for the chance she had given it, against all odds.

As Secret World has grown, many like-minded people who work hard to rescue and rehabilitate orphaned and injured wildlife have joined Pauline. Every animal, no matter how small, will always be given that second chance. Equally importantly, her charity is there to educate the public concerning the need to protect wildlife and the ways in which this can be done.

Their task is never-ending. Sadly there will always be more and more animals finding themselves in need of the kind of care that Secret World Wildlife Rescue offers. One can only hope that Pauline and her dedicated staff and volunteers will always be there to give an expert, helping hand.

Jason Venus

A couple of one-week-old leverets being syringe fed.

Andy Rouse

Brown hare – who's got big ears?

Hare or Rabbit?

There is often confusion – is it a hare? Or is it a rabbit? They are two totally different species.

Rabbit babies, known as kittens, are born blind, naked and deaf in an underground stop and are protected by their mothers. By the time they are fully furred and seen up above ground they are well on the way to being weaned.

Baby hares, known as leverets, are born above ground fully furred and with their eyes open. Left alone by their mothers, the young hares lie flat in the dips of the ground, called a form. They will often opt to freeze if found but are capable of running if danger is near.

Of course, the adult is easily recognised by its huge ears that have black tips. Both species only feed their young once or twice a day, so these orphans, if strong, are one of the few babies that don't have to be fed constantly throughout the day.

Three-week-old baby rabbit.

Rabbit enjoying the sun.

Simon Kidner

Colin Seddon

Above: *Stretching rabbit – life's a yawn.*

Right: *Bunny 1 and Bunny 2.*

Colin Seddon

Andy Rouse

Colin Seddon

Adult Hare – Easily recognised by its big ears...

Colin Seddon

...that have black tips on them.

Left: *Young leveret – 'Shhh! I'm not really here.'*

43

Wendy Turner-Webster

Television presenter and patron of Secret World

Colin Seddon

From my frequent visits to Secret World with the 'Pet Rescue' film crew, I have seen so many animals given love and care by Pauline Kidner and her dedicated team. To see the wild animals recovering and eventually being released is truly wonderful. Even the odd domesticated waif and stray has arrived and still received that individual TLC. I am proud to be their patron – long may Secret World continue!

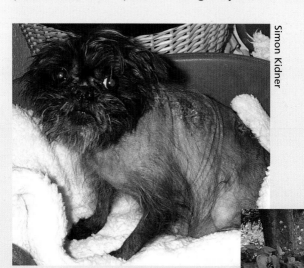

Simon Kidner

Many viewers followed the story of Pippa on 'Pet Rescue'. Dumped in a cardboard box outside the centre, almost completely bald and covered in sores, she was a sorry sight. Six months later she was a different dog. Pippa was to spend the rest of her life as a family pet at Secret World.

Simon Kidner

Richard Austin

Richard Austin

Abandoned in a carrier bag in a field, this very pretty kitten was lucky to be discovered by a farm worker. Secret World soon found a new home for her even though it's not meant to deal with domestic animals!

Jeff Searle

Max is a rescue dog who spends all her day following the staff around at the rescue centre, just hoping that someone is going to throw that ball!

Another rescue dog called Toby that came to live at Secret World with Nikki. 'Do something wrong, who me??!'

Paul Phillips/CFTWI

CFTWI

Wendy Turner-Webster is also Patron of Care For The Wild International (CFTWI) whose adoption programmes help care for animals all over the world. Their Adopt A Badger programme helps pay for much of the badger-care work carried out at Secret World. Here are some photographs of some of the other animals that can be adopted through this charity to help animals worldwide.

Orang-utan are the most endangered of the great apes, threatened by illegal logging, and poaching for the bushmeat and pet trades. CFTWI supports a rescue centre in Borneo, which is currently caring for over 200 orphaned orang-utans. The orang-utan require many years of dedicated care as they learn essential tree-climbing, foraging and building skills. A safe release site has been found for the apes, and rehabilitated orphans are being reintroduced back into the rainforest of Borneo, where they belong.

Wendy Turner-Webster is a foster parent to Aitong, one of the orphaned elephants on CFTWI's adoption programme. The programme supports the rescue and rehabilitation of orphaned elephants in Kenya. The orphans receive expert loving care, as they are gradually reintroduced into the wild herds of Tsavo East National Park. CFTWI also supports anti-poaching and de-snaring projects to ensure their long-term safety.

46

Photographs: CFTWI

There may be as few as 5000 tigers left in the wild, and without protection they could soon be lost for ever. Tigers are killed for their bones which are used in traditional medicines, and remaining populations are small and fragmented. CFTWI has an adoption programme for orphaned tigers in Cambodia and Laos. The programme supports the long-term care of tigers rescued from illegal trade as well as widespread anti-poaching projects, to protect the tigers left in the world.

Swans

It is sad that most swans come into our care thanks to injuries caused directly or indirectly by human activities. The majority that are admitted to Secret World do so as a result of having been shot, suffering from lead poisoning, having fishing hooks trapped in their necks or, all too often, having flown into power cables.

Often regarded as aggressive, they can be easily transported in special swan wraps – almost like a carrier bag! It is always a pleasure to return swans to the water when they recover from their ordeal.

Jason Venus

The most graceful of birds.

Above: *Cygnet – ugly duckling… I don't think so.*

Right: *Who wouldn't be proud of babies as pretty as these?*

Colin Fountain

49

Andy Rouse

It's amazing that such a large bird can be so graceful in flight.

Richard Austin

Simon Kidner

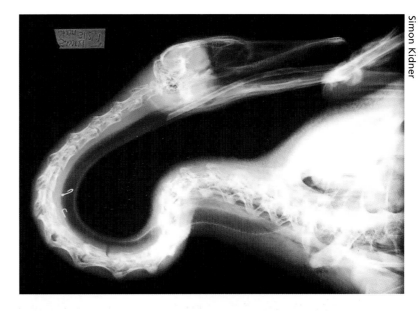

Simon Kidner

Nikki returns Sinker, who has recovered from his operation, to his pond at Unity Farm.

Top: *'Sinker' the cygnet was found in a poor condition with a fishing hook stuck in his beak. Further veterinary examination, including an X-ray showed two further hooks that had been ingested over a period of time.*

Above: *Sinker, despite his shaven neck, is happy to be back with family and friends.*

Nick Baker

Wildlife expert and television presenter

To have a healthy countryside there has to be a food chain from floor to ceiling! Creepy-crawlies, bugs, reptiles and amphibians all play a part in the survival of our bird and animal life, and indeed have a beauty of their own.

I know that Secret World will treat the smallest creature that comes into their care and will pass that respect on to their many visitors on the open days at this rescue centre. Children are allowed to pond dip but the greatest care is given to ensure that each bug is returned safely to the water to continue its life. Educational talks explain the fascinating side of snakes, lizards, frogs and toads. That's what it is all about – to look, learn and protect creatures and their habitat so that there will always be a beautiful countryside for future generations to enjoy.

Simon Kidner

Richard Taylor-Jones

Above: *Common newt.*

Left: *Pond dipping at one of the 'open weekends' at Secret World Wildlife Rescue.*

Above: *Common frog – Many people worry when their pond is full of frog-spawn that they will be inundated with adults. However, most are eaten by a wide variety of predators. It is worth remembering that frogs will always return to the pond where they were spawned. Along with toads they are very often casualties of grass-strimmers.*

Right: *Frog-spawn.*

Richard Taylor-Jones

Colin Fountain

Colin Fountain

Colin Seddon

Left: *The harmless grass snake's usual defences are to play dead or release a disgusting smell – it is unlikely to bite!*

Below: *They are often casualties after becoming caught in nets, especially if a frog has recently been devoured, which makes their body unusually wide. One of our rescues involved a snake that regurgitated three frogs, two of which revived – a hat-trick of rescues!*

Left: *Grass snake – and here's the guy who will be eating tadpoles and frogs. If you have a pond, then you probably have a grass snake who pays you regular visits. However, alerted by vibration, you will rarely see him or her as they will quickly slither away. Grass snakes are olive green with a colourful band just behind the head that can range from yellow or orange to red.*

Colin Fountain

Simon Kidner

Above: *A young visitor meets a snake for the first time at Secret World's 'Creepy-crawlie' open weekend, held each August Bank Holiday.*

Left: *Adder.   Our only venomous snake, and rarely seen, is easily recognised by it zigzag markings. Over 85 per cent of people bitten by adders were trying to kill them at the time. Shy and secretive, adders will usually retreat quicker than you.*

Jeff Searle

Colin Fountain

Above: *A legless lizard that will drop its tail if handled incorrectly. These can be another casualty of the grass-strimmer but also of the domestic cat.*

Left: *An escaped boa constrictor got more than he bargained for when he wrapped himself around a warm car exhaust on a stationary car. When the car continued its journey 'things became a little too hot' and a surprised car driver following the vehicle was amazed when an eight-foot boa dropped onto the road in front of her. Reported to the police, the snake was brought to Secret World and luckily had only sustained a dislocated jaw, four broken ribs and minor friction burns. This unusual guest, pictured with Ellie, made a full recovery and we were able to reunite him with his much-relieved owner. Although not the case in this instance, we are often called out to snakes that have been abandoned by their owners.*

Deer

Deer are probably the most difficult species of all to care for and rehabilitate. They are very nervous and shy creatures. Fawns, all too often, are picked up by people who don't realise that it is natural for them to be left quietly in the long grass waiting for their mother to return. There is nothing worse than being presented with a baby that, in your heart of hearts, you know should really have been left alone. It is so important, before picking up any wildlife baby to ensure that it is a true orphan. The golden rule is to leave them alone, as long as they are healthy and content, then return an hour or so later to see if they are still there. If the animal is calling and in obvious distress then it does need help and you must act.

Deer can die purely through stress and therefore in a crisis it is important to cover their heads (or ideally their whole body) with a coat or blanket. This reduces stress and contains body heat and you are then on the first step of recovery. Human contact must be kept to a minimum at all times.

Tiny fawns and kids need to have just one carer, who will have to spend a lot of time building up confidence with this tiny exquisite creature, in order to get it to feed.

Richard Austin

Colin Seddon

Far left: *Nikki caring for 'Spice' a very young roe-deer kid (two days old), who was retrieved by a dog whilst on a family walk. It is very important that dogs should be kept on leads during the months of May and June, when most deer are born and lie up in long grass.*

Left: *Every time a new species started to arrive at Secret World it was the start of learning 'what to do'.*

Above: *A 'full scale' of roe-deer kids being cared for at Secret World Wildlife Rescue – Doh (doe!), Ray, Me, Fah, Soh, Lah, Te, Doh(2), and Major.*

Left: *Treacle, a fallow fawn, is very different from roe-deer kids as this baby follows its mother from the moment it is born. It therefore needs constant attention and is not happy left on its own.*

Richard Austin

59

Photographs: Andy Rouse

A red stag in prime condition. This fellow will have to prove his strength in the autumn in order to retain his harem of 10–20 hinds. The rutting season is when those huge antlers will be used to fight with any rivals who dare to challenge him. It is nature's way of ensuring that the strongest animal will be allowed to breed and pass on his genes, to help give us a healthy countryside.

Muntjac deer are a species that has been introduced into our countryside after escaping from zoos. Not the prettiest of deer (!) – they are becoming more common in Somerset although we have only had a few in as casualties so far.

Photographs: Andy Rouse

Adult roe with antlers in 'velvet' – 'If you love them, let them go' is not just a sentimental remark. This adult male is a very large animal that needs plenty of space and should be part of its own group. He's built for speed...

...it almost looks like he can fly!

Andy Rouse

Wildlife photographer and noisy television personality

As an avid badger photographer I'd always wondered what they did before parading for me outside their setts. In the silence of the forest I'd hear the occasional scuffle and muffled noise from deep inside a sett, but could never find a way of seeing what was going on.

Then a friend of mine showed me an article about an animal sanctuary in Somerset that had 'The Bluebell Sett' – a unique underground badger sett. It was my first visit to Secret World and the first time that I met the Kidners. Pauline took me into the darkened viewing area of the sett, and there were the answers to all my questions about badgers under-ground – they were all fast asleep. In fact they were snoring their heads off.

Carefully I set up my equipment, occasionally watched by a sleepy eye, until the light began to fade from the sky outside. The sounds of scratching came from outside, which triggered everyone else to slowly wake up and join in the foraging feast themselves.

Then, after a last glance in my direction they were off, out into the twilight. For hours I sat and watched as they came back and forth doing badgery things: bringing in fresh bedding, squabbling and of course sleeping. It was a truly memorable experience and one that I repeated several times after; it was such a special treat.

For me Secret World has always been a welcoming place, with cheery smiles but always a dedication to animals that I admire. Calls come in at all hours of the night, yet Pauline and her team are always ready to respond, dashing out the door with a half-cup of coffee and some very bleary eyes. Secret World deserves our help, for it helps those that cannot help themselves, and what better cause is there than that?

Andy Rouse

Stacey the Stoat playing hide and seek –
a hand-reared orphan at Secret World.

Glade, a resident boar badger in the observation sett at Secret World Wildlife Rescue. A year after the death of Bluebell, Glade, an orphaned badger went through the rearing system at the centre. Despite being released, he remained too tame and was brought home to live there. He has a girlfriend called Tess who is also unable to be released owing to health problems, so they have each other for company.

Right: No, this picture is up the right way up! This badger is going down a sheer side to get a drink – just proving the tremendous muscles that they have in their necks and shoulders – pure power machines!

Photographs: Andy Rouse

65

Photographs: Andy Rouse

Rhino – To lie down underneath a Land Rover and have such a close encounter with a rhino is a truly amazing experience. She was a maximum of 5 feet from my head at all times and quizzically watched me changing film and fiddling with my camera. Not once did she show any aggressive tendencies, but I am experienced enough to know that this could change in an instant so I was always on my guard.

Left: Hippo – This is one of my all-time favourites, probably due to the lovely low light and the fact that I was actually sitting in the water with her. It was an awesome moment, the eye contact with me says it all and I knew that within seconds the world in front of me could be full of a hippo exploding through the water towards me. Fortunately all was calm.

Roe-deer – they are perhaps my favourite species in the UK to work with, a real passion. Always unpredictable, always turning up where you least expect them and always challenging me as a photographer. This particular shot was taken during the annual rut as a buck strutted through this poppy field looking for a female to court.

Bats

Bats are not the most popular of animals! When asked what species of bat we have in this country, the answer is usually fruit bats or vampire bats. Neither are to be found in Britain – all our bats are insect eaters so we are all quite safe. All 16 species of bats are to be found in Somerset as we have the ancient woodlands and caves which are so important for the hibernation of these flying mammals.

The two noctule bats pictured below were long-term residents at Secret World. Having spent fifteen years in captivity they were quite used to being shown to people by hanging them on the front of our sweaters. Once they had had enough they climbed up to the neckline and disappeared underneath to hang in the dark. We became quite famous for 'bats in the bra' especially as we keep baby bats in pouches under our clothes as they would normally have been carried by their mothers. They always seem happier if kept next to a heartbeat.

Photographs: Colin Seddon

Far left: *Male noctule bat – Himmy did not have the best of table manners. He would often shake his head whilst eating his supper of mealworms which resulted in remnants being flicked across the room!*

Left: *Female noctule bat – Liz Mullineaux, our vet, can proudly boast that she sterilised Bertha when discovering that she had cysts on her ovaries. Not bad when you consider this bat was only 6cms long. She went on to live a further two years.*

Richard Austin

Jason venus

Colin Fountain

Top left: *A juvenile pipestrelle bat being fed milk by an artist's brush. Even when fully grown he will only weigh the same as a 20p piece.*

Above: *Typical injury caused by a cat swiping the bat as it emerges from its roost. The tiny holes will stop the bat from flying. As long as no bones are broken, these holes will quickly heal and the bat will be released in a few days.*

Left: *Brown long-eared bat – one of the prettiest species.*

69

Pollyanna Pickering

One of Europe's foremost wildlife artists
The Pollyanna Pickering Foundation was established in 2001
to raise funds for conservation and disaster relief worldwide

My work as a wildlife artist has led me to become involved with birds and animals in every aspect of my life. For over fifteen years I ran a registered bird hospital from my home in the Peak District of Derbyshire, and cared for many hundreds of injured and orphaned creatures before re-releasing them into the wild. This gave my then teenaged daughter the most original excuses for being late at school – 'We had to collect an injured bat', 'I had to feed the leverets', or 'Our slow-worm just gave birth'!

Surprisingly, I never had a badger brought in to be cared for. You can imagine my delight the first time I visited Secret World to meet seven orphaned badger cubs being cared for in Pauline's kitchen/nursery. Within a very short time I had a sketchpad in one hand and a feeding bottle in the other, trying to encourage a squirming six-week-old youngster to drink.

My experiences running my own sanctuary have also given me a personal insight into the dedication and commitment needed to care for and rehabilitate wildlife, and I have the greatest admiration for the work done by Pauline, and all at Secret World, in caring for our precious and beautiful wildlife.

Study of a six week old badger cub
Very unsteady on his feet but trying a few
tentative steps — curious

Fur soft.

Polyanna Pickering

Baby badgers in Pauline's kitchen.

The Lucky Find

Eddie the Eagle Owl

Eddie the eagle owl was rejected by his mother and came to our centre at the tender of age of three weeks. Even then he was an impressive size although it belied a very gentle nature. Those huge orange eyes made him attractive to everyone and he was happy to sit back and take all the fuss. Sadly, he has not been the healthiest of birds and was to fall ill to a chest complaint that required daily doses of vapour medication.

Eddie was very patient and recovered with the tender loving care of Ellie West who took on the responsibility of his care as he grew. An X-ray of Eddie was necessary to see if his chest complaint had cleared, which luckily it had but the X-ray also showed that Eddie was an Edwina!

Photographs: Richard Austin

Eddie with Nikki – A very big ball of fluff even at four weeks old!

Ellie patiently administering vapour to clear Eddie's lung infection... or should we say Edwina!

Photographs: Richard Austin

Above: *Easy to see the bond between Ellie and Edwina – such a big bird with huge talons and yet Ellie knows that Edwina would never hurt her.*

Left: *Edwina sporting different coloured bandages on her feet after a minor operation.*

Doc Cox

Television personality, singer, banjo player, comedian, carrot…

I did quite a few unusual things during my 'That's Life' career. I sang at the Albert Hall with Esther Rantzen, I danced the boogaloo with 'Miss Whiplash' and I dressed as a giant cactus and chased tourists around Kew Gardens. Yet all of these mighty achievements pale into significance, when compared to the most astounding thing I ever did, which was to meet the badger cubs at Secret World.

Most of us only see badgers fleetingly in our headlights, vanishing into the dark hedgerows, or as tragic corpses on morning roadsides. Thanks to my friendship with Pauline Kidner and her wonderful League Of Super-Heroes at Secret World, I actually got to hold a badger cub and feed it. I was amazed at the amount of dinner that one tiny animal could throw around (my trousers and jacket will never be the same) but I wouldn't have missed it for all the world.

What Secret World is doing for all sorts of injured animals is wonderful, and Pauline and the gang are just about the most remarkable people I have ever met. (In fact, I've only ever met one person more remarkable, and he was small, black-and-white, hairy, and had disgraceful table manners.)

Secret World is a wonderful place, and the people who work there are extraordinary indeed.

In fact I'm so impressed by them, I wrote this deplorable poem. Try to ignore the awful rhymes, but please pay special attention to the bit about giving them money!

If you don't make a sound, then deep underground
Some fat, sleeping badgers you'll meet,
In a purpose built sett, a small maisonette
Double bedroom with bathroom ensuite.

There's one snoozing there, his feet in the air
His figure is portly, not trim,
He eats half the day then sleeps in the hay,
My God! How I wish I was him!

In the wild, wild West of England
Where The Severn hits the sea,
And the M5's covered in cow plop
That's where I long to be.

And the nicest bit is Somerset,
In fact I must declare
I once had a horse called Weston
'cos she was a Super Mare.

But in the big, bad world, the mad Min Of Ag world
The badger is threatened and though…
…a world with no badger in, is hard to imagerin
That's the challenge for Pauline and Co.

So let's come to the aid of the badger,
And let's keep a place in this land
For this creature omnivorous and O please deliver us
From a cruel world that won't understand.

And there in the Somerset Levels
Is a place I'll ne'er forget
A magic place, a Secret World,
Home of the Bluebell Sett.

Let's rally round for the badger.
Let's all lend a hand for old brock.
And as for Pauline Kidner, They oughta
spend a million quid on 'er
Thank you, yours faithfully Doc.

There, a wonderful woman called Pauline
And all her merry crew
Take care of birds and animals
(Would you care to sponsor a few?)

They rescue the injured and the orphans
And those who've been treated intolerably.
There's hedgehogs and rats, and squirrels and bats,
And barn owls and even a wallerably.

But the place is most famous for badgers
Come and see them and they'll be delighted.
At the front they are striped, in black and white
The same as Newcastle United.

Water Birds

In rehabilitation you often get the chance to see animals close up in a way that you would never have the opportunity to in the wild. This has to be weighed against the fact that often in the situation of rescue, you are going to be wading in waterways, through mud and usually in the coldest days of the year.

Still you can't have it all. Even when rescued many species have an endearing way of vomiting their food or ejecting faeces quite huge distances, all too often with that wonderful aroma of fish. Don't you wish that you worked with wildlife?!

Colin Fountain

Moorhen – a frequent wader seen in the many networks of waterways, called rhines, in Somerset. The young are balls of black fluff with bright-red beaks and gorgeous bright-blue eyebrows.

Vanessa Latford

Heron – Another bird often seen in our rhynes, after the eels. Watch that beak if you ever have to rescue one – it's just like a spear!

Above: Shelduck ducklings.

Right: *The very pretty shelduck that comes to the Bristol Channel to moult and breed. One of the few species where 'dad' plays a part in bringing up the young after they have been incubated. After about three weeks, the ducklings are collected into crèches on the water sometimes numbering up to 100. The male birds then protect the ducklings until they are about seven weeks old and able to fly.*

Colin Fountain

Colin Fountain

Simon Kidner

The mallard is not the most intelligent of ducks. So many decide to march their ducklings across the road having safely incubated them out under a hedge of someone's garden. They are not too fussed about seasons either. These two small orphaned ducklings (left) came into our centre in December!

81

Richard Austin

Dave Newman

Above: *Young grebe working his way through a 'starter' of whitebait.*

Left: *How many people can say they have shared their bath with a crested grebe?*

Vanessa Latford

Colin Seddon

Above: *Gannet adult with young.*

Left: *Herring gull.*

Right: *Cormorant, herring gull, guillemot, razorbill, whatever – each and everyone is important. If they need help, that's what we are here for.*

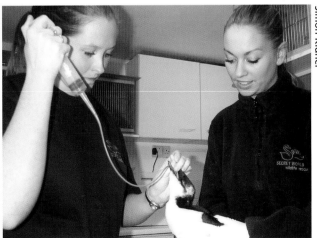

Simon Kidner

Andrew Lynford

(Alias Simon in Eastenders)
Actor, writer, singer and also patron of Secret World

Simon Kidner

Jason Venus

Secret World first became a part of my world in the spring of 1999. I was filming a series for ITV called 'Wild Thing' and it was during that time that Charcoal and Hope the badger cubs became personal showbiz chums! They went on to introduce me to friendly fox cubs and terrapins; pigs and bats; snakes and owls; and of course, Mr Woo, albino wallaby extraordinaire.

My lingering memory of him is that after his abandonment by his birth mother, he was carried in a rucksack by various Secret World surrogate parents to marvellous marsupial effect! When I was filming with Mr Woo, the director wanted him to hop along behind me whilst I was talking to the camera. He was brilliant – he obediently followed wherever I went and not once did he attempt to upstage. (Like he needed to with that cute face!) And now he has become Daddy Woo to a whole family.

As well as all the incredible creatures, I was lucky enough to meet Pauline too! And, of course, her amazing team of volunteers. I am always delighted to see how many people have affection for Secret World and its work, just as I do. One summer, I was invited to open the Hedgehog Rehabilitation Centre. (I know, it sounds like they all have terrible addictions but I am assured that's not the case!) So many people were there that day to lend their support.

People love Secret World and the wonderful work that is done by all who are associated with it. Long may it continue. Why not make it part of your world too?

Above left: *Andrew with baby Mr Woo.*

Left: *Pauline with the naked orphan.*

Photographs: Jason Venus

From incubator to rucksack, hanging on the door knob in the kitchen or riding around with Simon, Mr Woo became a firm favourite with everyone. His smart new fluffy coat was to make him even more attractive and Mr Woo became a 'star'. Appearing on 'Blue Peter' (he has his own 'Blue Peter' badge) and Disney Channel it was amazing he could still get in and out of his rucksack with such a big head!

As Mr Woo grew, he started to go outside in his pen, but still came in at night to laze in the armchair. Some people coming in from outside have to wipe their feet but...

Photographs: Purple Pictures

Nikki and Mr Woo – 'How do you do?'

'Oh, No! – I think I know where I'm going!'

'It was only a bit of mud – boys will be boys.'

'Guess I do look just that little bit smarter.'

...once fully grown, Mr Woo had to live permanently outside (although he still makes visits indoors even now!) so Mr Woo was given a friend – Mrs Woo!

Jeff Searle

It started with a kiss!

Jeff Searle

Colin Fountain

Mr Woo may look more interested in his crisps but after Baby Boo was born, we sent him off to the vets to be neutered. Obviously not quickly enough as the following year Mrs Woo and Baby Boo had joeys in their pouches – so Roo and Sue joined the group. It has all been sorted – we are stopping at five!

Mrs Woo and Baby Boo.

Murray

Andrew Gell

Murray was rescued by Pauline as a very small puppy. Bald from having mange, and bandy from malnutrition, he wasn't a pretty sight. He was to grow into a fine Alsatian-cross Doberman whose gentle nature made him a friend to so many orphans. Befriended by young fawns, he would lick them clean and encourage them to feed. Pauline's shadow; wherever Pauline is – Murray is never far away.

Richard Austin

Murray with Dudley – Friendship can sometimes just go too far!

Photographs: Richard Austin

Above: *Murray with Ebony, the badger cub – 'Come on – surely you're not that tired?'*

Right: *Murray with Mr Woo.*

Friends together – Pauline with Dot the red deer, Murray, Catkin the badger cub and a rabbit named Alice.

Jason Venus

Richard Austin

Professional photographer

Years ago I was sent by my editor to Secret World to photograph Pauline Kidner with a sick and injured tortoise. It was all of seventeen years ago, and since then I must have photographed hundreds of birds and animals at the sanctuary which speaks volumes for the animal welfare Secret World provides. The amount of animals that have been treated, loved, looked after and released back into the wild is a testament to Pauline and her staff whose knowledge and experience of treating sick animals is second to none. If it were at all possible for the animals to show their gratitude they would have made Pauline a saint by now.

Richard Austin

Far left: *Orphan fruit bats.* Richard Austin

Left: *Sally-Ann, a young Yorkshire terrier belonging to Pauline's mum.*

Photographs: Richard Austin

Above: *Three young fox cubs think life's a yawn – safe now they have been rescued.*

Left: *Nikki with a tortoise line-up – ready, steady, slow!*

Photographs: Richard Austin

Robbie the runt and Lizzie the lamb became firm friends as orphans in Pauline's kitchen. I am no longer surprised at what I might see in Pauline's kitchen, anything's possible – badgers, deer, bats, piglets, wallabies...

Helping Hands for Wildlife – It says it all –
That's what Secret World Wildlife Rescue is all about.

Above: *Gale, a twenty-four-hour old badger cub that survived and was eventually released, with a new family later in the year.*

Far left: *Tufty the baby squirrel.*

Left: *Stacey the orphan stoat.*

Birds of Prey

Why is it that birds of prey, buzzards, sparrowhawks, whatever, are so often the hated species because of their lifestyle, and yet talk about owls and people love them. Those big eyes win people over every time and yet they are just as efficient at catching their prey – they just do it at night when we don't see!

If brought into care, these birds must be fed on whole food that contains fur, feather and bone to allow them to digest their food and they then cast pellets made from the indigestible matter.

When Pauline first cared for Sage, her first barn owl, she had to buy in dead day-old chicks. It was not too difficult as defrosted, the chick would be eaten whole by the owl for dinner. However, when Pauline was presented with some barn owl chicks, they still needed to be fed on whole food but in very small pieces. Feeling rather squeamish at the thought of cutting up the dead chicks, Pauline had the brilliant idea of putting them in to a food processor – not such a good idea as the eyes and legs don't break down and the sight of them flailing around in the bowl did not help the situation. She went back to using a knife!

Not everything about caring for wildlife is pleasant – but to see these birds take to the wing when recovered has to be one of the best sensations that any rehabilitator can wish for.

Richard Austin

Tic, Tac and Toe, three orphaned tawny owls.

Jason Venus

Jo, the tawny owl. Injured in a road traffic accident, Jo came to us to recuperate for a few weeks. Three days after she arrived, a male tawny came and courted her every night. He would sit patiently on the tele-graph pole and call to her through the night. When she was completely fit, we waiting for him to come and opened the door of the aviary. Within minutes she had joined him and they flew away. We never saw them again.

Richard Austin

Simon Kidner

This peregrine falcon came in having been found collapsed in a field with an infection to an injury on his wing. Once treated and recovered, he was returned to his territory and given his freedom.

98

Jason Venus

Left: *Double trouble – two juvenile buzzards.*

Below: *Even while enjoying his meal, this buzzard is still on the lookout.*

Andy Rouse

Andy Rouse

It's so easy to miss this little owl sitting perfectly still against the tree for camouflage. The smallest of our owls, they have fantastic Denis Healey eyebrows!

Jeff Searle

Simon with Amber the female kestrel. Stolen by some children from the nest when she was very young, Amber was not fed correctly and is very small for her age. Kept in a canary cage, she has never learnt how to be wild and how to hunt for her food. We now use her for talks to make sure that this kind of thing will not happen again.

Vanessa Latford

Young barn owl. 'Leave me alone – I belong in the wild!'

Vanessa Latford

1st – TV Times Wildlife Photographic Competition 1992
Best of Tendring Landscape competition – 2nd 1995, 1st 1996, 1st 1997, 2nd 1998
Exhibited at Colchester Library and Essex Wildlife Trust

I have been photographing wildlife for approximately thirteen years, taking it a bit more seriously after winning a photographic competition in the *TV Times* and winning a trip to Kenya. I have a particular passion for mammals, with badgers and foxes being the favourites: also a growing fascination for whales, but I enjoy all aspects of the natural world.

I always try to time my visits each year to Secret World around the time of the badger cubs in Pauline's kitchen but my most exciting visit had to be when Oscar, the otter cub was being cared for by Nikki Hawkins. It takes a certain kind of dedication to feed badger cubs through the night, but I take my hat off to Nikki. Anyone who can get up in the middle of the night to feed an otter cub on fish soup has to be really keen or slightly crazy!

As surrogate mum, Nikki was to slowly wean the cub and even teach him to swim (in Pauline's bath!) before it was time for him to go outside into a rehabilitation pen. It is hard to understand how so much love can be lavished on such a small animal and then for the carer to be able to let them go back in to the wild. But as I have heard both Pauline and Nikki say so many times, if you love them, you will let them go – they need to live life to the full in the way that nature destined them to do. That really is love.

Eight-week-old otter cubs being syringed with fish/milk soup.

Vanessa Latford

Richard Austin

Richard Austin

Above: *Oscar enjoying life in luxury after being found running terrified across the A303 near Exeter. Otter cubs need to be reared by one person to keep them wild so that they can be set free when old enough.*

Far left and left: *Nikki was to be 'mum' for Oscar until weaned. That meant feeds and cuddles day and night – tiring for both of them!*

Richard Austin

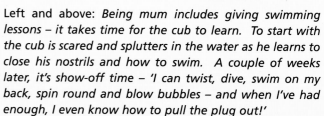

Richard Austin

Left and above: *Being mum includes giving swimming lessons – it takes time for the cub to learn. To start with the cub is scared and splutters in the water as he learns to close his nostrils and how to swim. A couple of weeks later, it's show-off time – 'I can twist, dive, swim on my back, spin round and blow bubbles – and when I've had enough, I even know how to pull the plug out!'*

Colin Seddon

Eighteen months later, Oscar takes a look from his release holt. It's up to him now – he's got to find his own fish, a new home and maybe a mate. Secret World has done as much as they can. Good luck!!

Colin Seddon

Above: *Have you seen that distinctive 'v' in the water as the otter swims with his nose just above the water?*

Left: *Have you seen how two minutes after coming out of the water, the otter can shake and look practically dry?*

LUCKY YOU!!

Photographs: Vanessa Latford

Above: *The erythristic badger – I knew him from when he was an eight-week-old cub and named him Eric. But over a time when he was about two years old, he began to approach me before I could get the camera out of the bag. He developed a bond between us that none of the other badgers did – taking peanuts from my hand. I particularly like this picture because of the lighting (a flash set up behind him that highlights his hair).*

Left: *Eric alongside a normal (melanistic) coloured badger.*

The sleeping fox – this was a rescued fox that couldn't be released. He was a very attractive fox, but just found having his photo taken, just a bit boring, and it became difficult to get his attention!

Photographs: Vanessa Latford

Above: *Fin back whale – I went on a whale research project in the Gulf of St Lawrence, Canada. This was the first time out on the water, and we were told this was an Ooh! Aaah! Day to prepare for the excitement of seeing whales.*

In fact this was the best time ever, out on the water. The water was like a pond and all the krill were jumping on the surface. The fin back whales were just trawling along on the surface with their mouths open. An amazing experience.

Left: *Killer whale/ orca – This was taken in Vancouver Island near Victoria. The boat stopped before the pod reached us, and its pot-luck how close the orcas go past. I was lucky to get this adult male, whose dorsal fin is much larger than the females.*

Below: *Grey whale – This grey whale was photographed in Baja Mexico at Magdalena Bay. This is where the grey whales come to give birth in the warm waters, then come late March, they migrate to the coast of Alaska.*

Photographs: Vanessa Latford

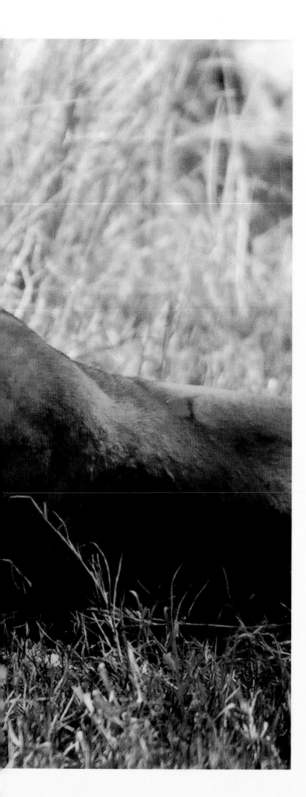

Lions – photographed on a private ranch in Kenya. We spent half an hour watching the mother and almost-grown cubs.

Badger Cubs

Pauline's kitchen has to be the one that most people will recognise from the many programmes that have shown the little black and white orphans that come to live there every spring. Known affectionately as the 'kitchen crew', these tiny cubs will arrive anytime after the end of January. There are many reasons why they become orphaned – sometimes their mothers have been killed on the roads, others cubs are discarded on the side of setts by diggers that have taken away the adults for baiting.

They often arrive cold, hungry and very, very frightened. These cubs that have to be bottle feed, sometimes as often as every hour will live in the kitchen until they are weaned. 'It's a bit like having puppies around, they are fantastic fun but a lot of hard work too,' said Pauline. 'Once there is another cub for company, they will only be handled when they are fed. They are left to interact with each other as we don't want them to get too tame.'

The 'kitchen crew' can number up to eight cubs, but many other weaned badger cubs come in to the centre, which has specialised indoor and outdoor pens to cope with them. Every year, over 50 cubs are cared for at Secret World. Mixed into family units, safe release sites are found for them and they are usually back in the wild by the time they are nearly a year old.

Simon Kidner

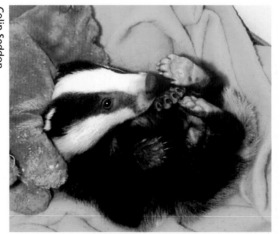

Colin Seddon

Eight-week-old badger cubs. Charcoal (left) enjoys a gentle game while Bilberry (right) is just too comfy to bother to move!

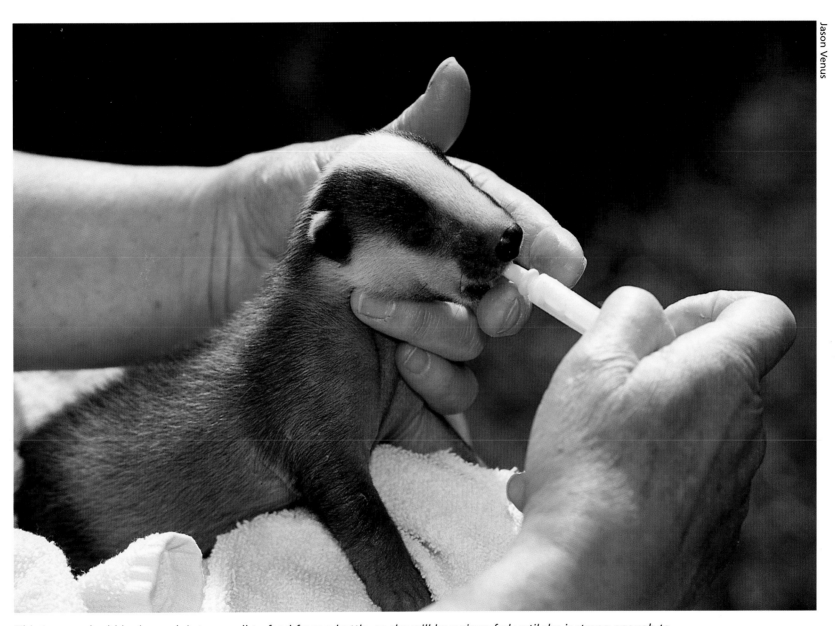

Jason Venus

This two-week-old badger cub is too small to feed from a bottle, so she will be syringe fed until she is strong enough to suck from a bottle.

Jason Venus

Pauline at feeding time – there is no such thing as manners when it comes to who gets fed first!

The 'kitchen crew' experience their first walk in the fields.

Colin Seddon

Colin Seddon

Colin Seddon

Jason Venus

Top: *In the outside pens, hay bags and tunnels give them plenty to play with.*

Above: *Sitting on his haunches, this 'teenager' is having a good old scratch.*

Top: *Who's watching who?*

Above: *We are always on the lookout for new release sites for our badgers.*

Colin Seddon

Remember the tiny badger cub on the front of this book? Well here she is, Gale as a young adult – her last photograph before being released. Arriving at only twenty-four hours old, she was fed every hour day and night for several weeks and even then bottle fed until weaned at sixteen weeks. Then it was outside into a grassed paddock with other badger friends to learn how to forage and slowly revert to being wild.

It is worthwhile – every hour of work and every pound that it cost, she made it.

Valerie Singleton

'Blue Peter', travel writer, presenter and patron of Secret World

I first became aware of Secret World through a badger knocked down on a road and needing care. Since then my involvement has lead me to become a patron to this nationally acclaimed rescue centre. I have to admit the hedgehog is my favourite and I have enjoyed visiting and seeing adult hedgehogs being given the best care but also tiny baby hoglets needing many feeds through the day and night.

Life at Secret World is very similar to mine. 'Blue Peter' gave me many challenges: involvement with animals and sometimes the programme included doing some zany things. Obviously at Secret World there is plenty of hands-on with animals but there is also the constant need to catch people's attention to raise funds whether it is to dress in animal costumes or running of marathons.

As a travel writer and presenter, I know how everyone thinks how wonderful it is to visit all those lovely countries but indeed it is often hard work. Similarly, working with animals looks fun but it is a tremendous commitment that brings happy and sad times.

And certainly as ex-presenter of the 'Money Programme', I know the serious side of Secret World. The ever-needed funds must keep coming in for them to continue their work. I sincerely hope that Secret World Wildlife Rescue will get all the support that they need, for the sake of the thousands of animals that benefit from their help every year.

Simon Kidner

Newborn hedgehog with its very first white spines just starting to sprout through.

118

Jason Venus

Above: *Several hours later, all the white spines are through on this group of 'pincushions'!*

Right: *Five weeks old and starting to lap, this baby is doing fine.*

Colin Seddon

Jason Venus

Simon Kidner

Above: *Albino hedgehog with pink eyes.*

Right: *'Blonde' hedgehogs can also be nearly white but they have blue eyes – just as cute!*

Andy Rouse

Our normal-coloured hedgehog showing their lovely brown face with the long pointed snout for rooting out insects. When fully grown, a hedgehog will have between and 3000 and 5000 spines.

Richard Austin

Above: *Sadly this little guy was used as a football by a group of school children. This is why we feel it is so important for us to go to schools to teach children about our wildlife.*

Left: *Well, this one made it, but sadly, all too often, they don't.*

Jason Venus

Jason Venus

The wildlife work was slowly draining the resources of the Secret World tourist attraction. With a poor trading season due to wet weather and the petrol shortage in 2000, there was not enough money to carry the centre through the winter and it had to close. There was a public outcry for the wildlife work to continue and with the support of the general public, the charity took over the centre and has worked hard continuing to care for injured wildlife.

It was a very tough time when difficult decisions had to be made. Within the charity mission, we were unable to keep the commercial animals like the cows, sheep, pigs and poultry so homes had to be found for them all. It was a very sad time for us all, but it has enabled us to focus on the care of the wild animals and to improve our care facilities for them.

So how do we raise enough money to carry on our work? Well, we do have five open week-ends a year and with the help of many hard-working volunteers we do all sorts! We try our best to get people to donate, adopt an animal, become a supporter or help with fund-raising. Christmas has us dressing up as Santa's elves – even the hedgehog has joined in!

Colin Seddon

Give him a wave – Mr Badger has come to town-oh! And yes please, drop a coin in the box – thanks!

Burnham Times

Jason Venus

Above: *Simon Kidner even ran the marathon in consecutive years.*

Left: *Brean Leisure Parks sponsor Secret World Wildlife Rescue in 2003 – launched with Andrew Lynford and Clinton Rogers (BBC news reporter).*

Simon Kidner

Everyone enjoys the ferret racing – nobody more then the ferrets! 'Double your money if you chose the winning ferret.' And if you lose, well never mind, you go away with a lovely warm feeling knowing that your money has gone towards the wildlife rescue at Secret World.

Barn Owls

We are pleased to have Mr Chris Sperring MBE as another patron of our centre. Chris who works for the Hawk and Owl Trust has been responsible for the improvement of large areas of farmland to support the barn owl and we are fortunate to have a good population of them in our area.

Ouch!, pictured below, was a very lucky barn owl indeed. Caught in the draught of the traffic, a vehicle clipped his leg as he tried to fly away. The leg was broken and he fell to the ground. Somebody nearby was able to retrieve him quickly from the road before he was run over by the busy traffic. And he was brought to Secret World.

Our vet was able to pin the leg and Ouch! made a complete recovery. Ellie's face says it all, as she releases him.

Simon Kidner

Ouch! the barn owl with broken leg.

Left: *Ellie releasing Ouch! the barn owl.*

Below: *'Second chance'.*

Photographs: Richard Austin

Foxes

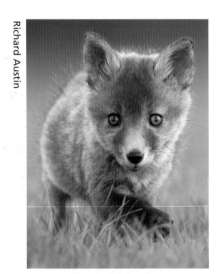

Richard Austin

Foxes are rarely happy in captivity and are often quite seriously ill before you can manage to catch them. They are very wary and as cubs, when chocolate-brown, have been mistaken for kittens or puppies, even by members of the veterinary profession!

We often hear about the horrible fox 'who ate my chickens', usually to find on further investigation the person concerned had actually forgotten to shut the chickens up in the first place or that the condition of the chicken house was less than secure.

Fox cubs look very pretty and, sadly, sometimes people think they will make good pets. As soon as the cub starts to eat solids, the distinct aroma of fox becomes very noticeable and all of a sudden, the pretty pet is no longer wanted! Unfortunately if a fox is too tame, it is impossible to release as it will approach people and will very soon be dispatched.

It is really important that foxes are cared by organisations that will return them to the wild.

Above: *An inquisitive fox cub.*

Right: *When first born, fox cubs are chocolate brown. They don't start to turn red until they are five to six weeks old.*

Jason Venus

Vixen with juvenile – so much to learn in order to survive.

Simon Kidner

Left: *There is no reason why a fox, or any wild animal for that matter, shouldn't receive treatment for injuries. They have the right to fluid therapy, antibiotics and pain relief, as with any other animal.*

Below left: *The biggest expense is keeping casualties contained whilst receiving treatment and medication. Not that we get many pole-vaulting foxes – but they can get through the smallest of holes!*

Below: *Home again – another success!*

Jason Venus

Colin Seddon

Richard Taylor-Jones

Jason Venus

Above: *Pauline with one of her original foxes, Gordon. He came to Secret World with his brother Bennet. They had been reared as pets and kept in a small pen. We were able to give them more space and they became firm favourites with the visitors. It's not often that you see a fox greeting you by wagging its tail!*

Left: *A glimpse is usually all you will get of the wary fox.*

Chris Packham

Wildlife Expert, writer, television presenter and patron of Secret World

Anon

Many people like animals, some care about them more than most, some it could fairly be said 'love' them; thank goodness for that. Much, if not most, of our wildlife has a tough time these days, and the kind of support that Secret World offers creatures in crisis is fantastic. As you probably know, badgers have always been a bit of a speciality for the staff at SW and have been so for myself as well. I began researching several clans in the 1970s when I was a teenager, got into a full-blown study at university and very nearly began a PhD on the by then dreaded nocturnal blighters. Yes, I'd all but had it with badgers! Whilst my mates and their girlfriends were down the pub I was in the woods getting bitten by insects, or worse, in the lab analysing dung. I analysed dung every week for four years. That's a lot of dung – I needed some serious drinking time!

Nevertheless, I forgave and forgot and have been 'badgery' for years, always keen to see what sneaks out of the sett, and stay in touch with these extraordinary animals' problems. And it's not easy for them. One minute they are on the T-shirt or the television, the next on a 'Wanted' poster or being paraded as a pest. There is still a lot to find out about badgers, but learning to live with them and work out compromises is an essential direction of effort, and in this field the Secret World team have been a pioneer. But then it's not all about science, its also about sensitivity and compassion and there's never been any short-age of that down in Highbridge at Secret World Wildlife Rescue.

Colin Seddon

Carey and one of her three cubs. She was found very ill near a barn where she had only just given birth. Brought back to the centre, Carey recovered with a course of antibiotics and continued to care for her cubs. She was released later in the year with her family.

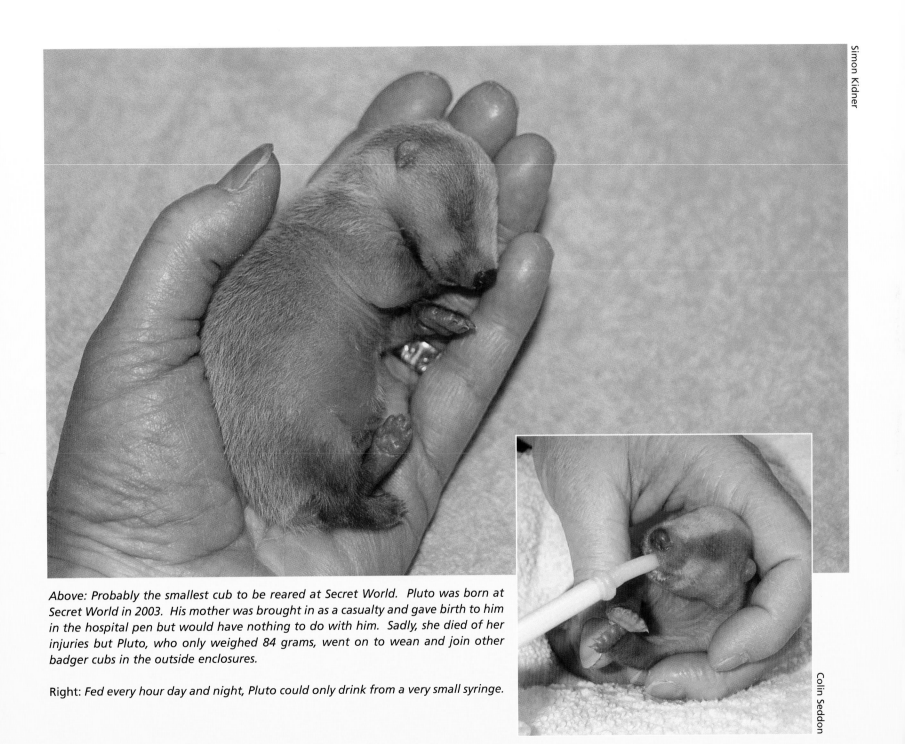

Simon Kidner

Above: Probably the smallest cub to be reared at Secret World. Pluto was born at Secret World in 2003. His mother was brought in as a casualty and gave birth to him in the hospital pen but would have nothing to do with him. Sadly, she died of her injuries but Pluto, who only weighed 84 grams, went on to wean and join other badger cubs in the outside enclosures.

Right: *Fed every hour day and night, Pluto could only drink from a very small syringe.*

Colin Seddon

133

David Higgs

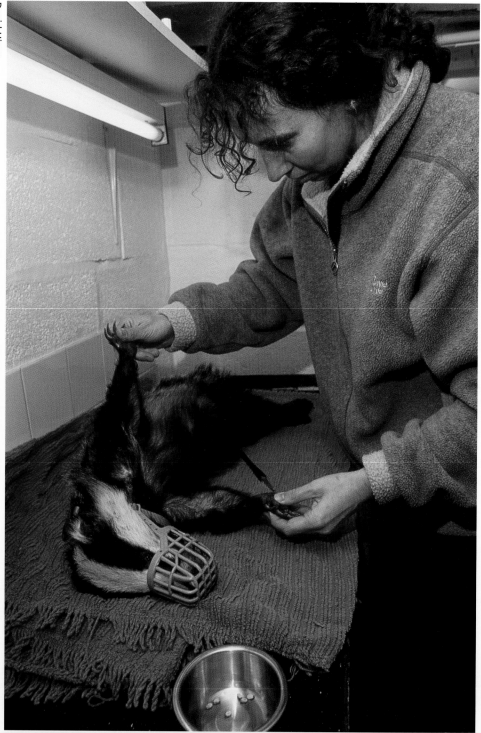

Jason Venus

Secret World Wildlife Rescue is very lucky to have vet Liz Mullineaux at Quantock Veterinary Hospital in Bridgwater to complement their dedicated team. Liz has worked with Secret World for many years and has done much for the rehabilitation of all wildlife but particularly badgers. Together with other very experienced vets, she has edited a manual, available to all veterinary practices, that includes every single wildlife species to be found in Great Britain.

It now means that there is information available on the lifestyle of the animal, natural parameters, common injuries and ailments, and drugs available that are compatible. The book also explains methods of after-care and release.

Working together, Secret World Wildlife Rescue and the Quantock Veterinary Hospital will ensure that every animal will be given the best possible care.

Chris Packham

Who needs tigers? Celebrity exotics from far-flung places are no match for the fox next door. Just look! He is exquisite, and after all my travels and encounters with the world's great beasts he can still make my heart miss a beat in my own backyard. That's entertainment!

135

Photographs: Chris Packham

More birds than sky! The best things in life are... birds, and here are 40,000 lesser snow geese honking over a wintry New Mexico reserve. Sometimes it's best not to reach for the camera when a spectacle's on, but this time I did.

Simple symphony of the commonplace. There is a field near my house which flowers like this most years and for days it is a postcard of heaven. It seems quintessentially English, timeless and looks better than any Monet I've ever seen. Keep your water lilies... I've got my buttercup!

A Big Thank You!

There is one name that appears too many times in this book and it is mine! The creation of Secret World and its work has only been made possible thanks to a very understanding husband and a family that have been prepared too often to be neglected.

It has also only succeeded because of the dedicated staff and volunteers who have given hours of their time to care for all our patients.

And as a charity, it is only the donations from members of the public that allow us to carry out our work. You have been part of this by purchasing our book as the royalties will go to the work at Secret World Wildlife Rescue.

To all of you – a big thank you. You are all stars that have made the little bit of heaven known as Secret World possible.

Pauline B

Colin Fountain

Stan Dean

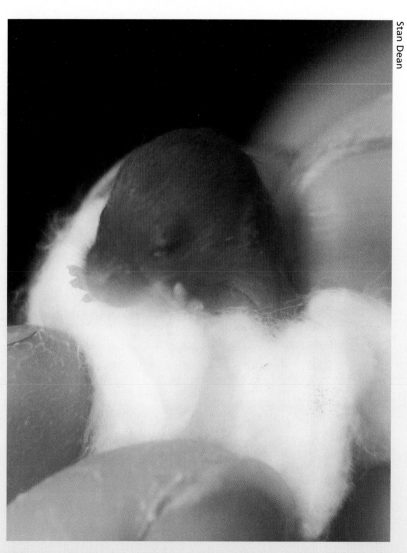

Spider monkey – in this life you meet other people dedicated to animals too. This tiny baby was reared by Maria Fountain. What did it entail? Two years of body contact, that's all! With her all day, slept with her at night and when it came to having a bath? – sat on her head!

Minute! – this tiny vole wrapped in cotton wool had to be fed by a tiny artist's brush. Fed every two hours it's easy to look after if you are a woman. You just take it with you wherever you go, tucked down your bra, and if you have a tiny bottle of milk down there as well, it's just the right temperature when needed!

Like to know more about Secret World Wildlife Rescue?

Visit our website on
www.secretworld.org

or email
enquiries@secretworld.org

This wildlife charity helps care for over 3000 casualties every year. Running purely on donations, the centre works twenty-four hours a day, seven days a week, offering advice, collecting casualties and reducing pain and suffering through nursing and care.

We eventually hope to fulfil our long-term project to have our own wildlife hospital which will further improve the care and success of rehabilitation of wildlife at our centre. Even so, each and every casualty, no matter how small or large they may be, is always given individual attention with the aim of returning them to the wild.

Would you like to become a supporter? Maybe adopt a hedgehog, bat or badger? Perhaps you would like to visit on one of our open days and see Secret World for yourself. For more information please contact:

Secret World Wildlife Rescue
New Road
Highbridge
Somerset
TA9 3PZ

Telephone: 01278 783250
Fax: 01278 793109

Drawn by Phil Reddish

Artists impression of the barn conversion at Secret World Wildlife Rescue which one day we hope will be our new wildlife hospital.

Our unique adoptions make the perfect gift for animal lovers of all ages!

Hedgehog Adoption

By adopting these wonderful animals, you will be directly helping us with our twenty-four-hour, seven-days-a-week hedgehog rescue and rehabilitation project. In a typical year we look after at least 400 hedgehogs – rescue work we can only do with the help of our supporters. As a Secret World Hedgehog Adopter you will receive one of these packs:

SINGLE: £18.00
A beautiful photo of a rescued hedgehog, your own adoption certificate, a species information fact-sheet and two of our very popular Secret World newsletters a year.

FAMILY: £24.00
A wonderful way to involve all the family. A beautiful photo of a rescued hedgehog, your family adoption certificate, a species information fact-sheet and two of our very popular Secret World newsletters a year.

Bat Adoption

By adopting these secretive animals, you will be directly helping us with our twenty-four-hour, seven-days-a-week bat rescue and rehabilitation project. We treat bats for all manner of injuries and also rear many orphans – rescue work we can only do with the help of our supporters. As a Secret World Bat Adopter you will receive one of these packs:

SINGLE: £18.00
A beautiful photo of a rescued bat, your own adoption certificate, a species information fact-sheet and two of our very popular Secret World newsletters a year.

FAMILY: £24.00
A wonderful way to involve all the family. A beautiful photo of a rescued bat, your family adoption certificate, a species information fact-sheet and two of our very popular Secret World newsletters a year.

Badger Adoption

By adopting a badger, you will help the many badgers young and old that come into the care of Secret World Wildlife Rescue. Every year, over a hundred badgers are taken into the expert care of Pauline Kidner and her staff at the rescue centre in Somerset. As a Secret World Badger Adopter you will receive one of these packs:

PACK A: £15.95
A certificate with a colour picture, a cuddly badger (size 15cm), a badger fact-sheet, a window-sticker, an update after six months.

PACK B: £24.95
A certificate with a colour picture, the video 'Badgers in my Kitchen', a badger fridge magnet, a badger fact-sheet, a window-sticker, an update after six months.

We need your support...

Richard Austin

Baby dormice.

By becoming a supporter of Secret World, you are helping care for over 3000 wildlife casualties during the year. A presentation pack with a personal certificate makes this an attractive gift for everyone, of all ages. Receive the newsletters telling you all the stories of the many rescued animals that eventually return to the wild. A gift that can be given or received in the knowledge that orphaned and injured wildlife will gain a 'second chance'. Your support helps us to help animals that can not help themselves.

MEMBERS: £18.00

As a member you will receive two copies of our popular Secret World newsletter packed with up-to-the-minute news on our animal rescue and rehabilitation work and a Special Invitation to Secret World open days.

FAMILY MEMBERS: £24.00

A wonderful opportunity to involve the whole family in the care and protection of our precious wildlife. Family members receive all the benefits above plus a signed photo of Pauline with one of the animals rescued by Secret World.

FOUNDERS' CIRCLE: £250

An opportunity to become really close to the work of Secret World. In addition to the full membership benefits, 'Founders' Circle' supporters will receive a signed book from Pauline and your name will be engraved on a plaque in the grounds of the rescue centre, plus you will be invited to a Special VIP tour of Secret World once a year with Pauline.

LIFE MEMBERS: £500

An increasingly popular way of showing support for our animal rescue work. One payment will entitle you to all the above membership benefits, plus our heartfelt thanks.

To adopt a hedgehog, bat or badger or to become a supporter of Secret World please call us on 01278 783250

Additional Books and Videos

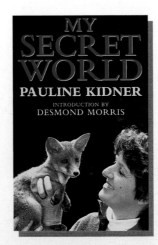

My Secret World book
(Softback)

The love that Pauline has for her animals comes through on every page and there are plenty of lovely photographs to enjoy.

£7.99 (Code: SW0002)

Glade's Journey book
(Softback)

In her slightly crazy existence with animals everywhere, Pauline's wicked sense of humour shines through in this wonderfully warm book.

£7.99 (Code: SW0003)

Badgers in My Kitchen
(Video)

A chance to see what it is really like to have badgers in your kitchen, and many other animal stories to enjoy.
Running time approx. 60 mins.

£9.99 (Code: SW0004)

Secret World
(Video)

A behind-the-scenes look at the work of this badger and wildlife rescue centre run by Pauline Kidner and her dedicated staff.
Running time approx. 60 mins.

£9.99 (Code: SW0005)

SPECIAL OFFER! Order 1 book with 1 video for only £12.99
(offer applies to the above 4 titles only)

To order any of the above titles
or additional copies of
Exploring the SECRET WORLD of Wildlife Rescue (£14.95)
please call us on **01278 783250**